LIBERALS AND PROGRESSIVES seem to thrive on crises. They are, in any case, unusually proficient in creating or calling attention to them, often as excuses to impose new taxes and regulations or to gain additional power and influence for themselves. In the 1960s they gave us the "poverty crisis" and the "urban crisis," followed in the 1970s and 1980s by the "environmental crisis," the "energy crisis," and the "homeless crisis." Later we had the "health care crisis" and, more recently, the civilization-threatening "global-warming crisis." None of these ever qualified as a genuine crisis, if by that term we mean a moment of danger that must be navigated by wise statesmanship or effective policy. Some have found it useful to turn multifaceted problems into crises in order to stampede the public into adopting policies it would otherwise (quite sensibly) reject.

Today the issue of the hour is the "inequality crisis," another overhyped issue that is being seized upon as an excuse to raise taxes, attack "the rich," and discredit policies that

[

D1298303

gave us three decades of prosperity, booming real estate and stock markets, and an expanding global economy. For several years, ever since the financial crisis of 2008, journalists and academics have been turning out books and manifestos bearing such titles as *The New Gilded Age; The Killing Fields of Inequality; The Great Divergence: America's Growing Inequality Crisis and What We Can Do About It;* and *The Price of Inequality: How Today's Divided Society Endangers Our Future,* to list just a few of the many dozens of works on the subject that have appeared of late. The common message of these books is not subtle: the rich have manipulated the political system to lay claim to wealth they have not earned and do not deserve, and they have done so at the expense of everyone else.

In the past, those who wrote about inequality focused on poverty and the challenge of elevating the poor into the working and middle classes. No more. Today they are preoccupied with the rich and with schemes to redistribute their wealth downward through the population. Many of the new egalitarians – professors at Ivy League universities, well-paid journalists, or heirs to family wealth – are well-off and comfortable by any reasonable standard. In interpreting their complaints about "the rich" or the top "1 percent," one naturally thinks of Samuel Johnson's barbed comment about the reformers of his day: "Sir," he said, "your levelers wish to level down as far as themselves; but they cannot bear leveling up to themselves." There is a sense in this controversy that we are watching members of the top 2 percent or 3 percent of the income distribution perform class warfare against the top 1 percent, while everyone else looks on from a distance, apparently convinced that the new class struggle has little to do with their own circumstances.

THE PIKETTY BUBBLE

The controversy over inequality gathered additional steam in recent weeks with the publication of Thomas Piketty's new book,

Capital in the Twenty-First Century (Belknap/ Harvard University Press), a dense and data-filled work of economic history running to nearly 700 pages that makes the case against

---

There is a sense in this controversy that we are watching members of the top 2 percent or 3 percent of the income distribution perform class warfare against the top 1 percent.

---

inequality far more extensively and exhaustively than any work that has appeared heretofore. His book, published in March 2014, climbed to the top of the best-seller lists by mid-April, where it remained for several weeks thereafter. Bookstores in New York City, Washington, D.C., and Boston quickly sold out of copies, and even Amazon could not keep up with public demand for the book. The Piketty "phenomenon" arrived as a surprise to just about everyone, most especially to the publisher. "We've printed and printed and printed, and the market soaks up whatever we print," the book's editor at Harvard University Press said in April, just a few weeks after the publication date. "The American reception of the book has re-energized interest in France. Now the French edition is sold out." The editor was not complaining; this is the kind of problem publishing houses like to have.

All this attention quickly turned Piketty, a scholarly-looking professor at the Paris School of Economics, into something of a literary celebrity and his treatise into a rallying point for those favoring income redistribution and higher taxes for the rich. *The New York Times* called the author "the newest version of a now-familiar specimen: the overnight intellectual sensation whose stardom reflects the fashions and feelings of the moment." Paul Krugman, in a review essay in *The New York Review of Books*, called the book "magnificent" and "awesome." Martin Wolf of the *Financial Times* described it as "extraordinarily important," while a reviewer for *The Economist* suggested that Piketty's book is likely to change the way we understand the past two centuries of economic history. A columnist for the *Financial Times* called the mass of commentary surrounding the book a "Piketty bubble." Meanwhile, *The Spectator* in London helpfully offered tips to people wishing to bluff their way to appearing well informed about the book without having taken the trouble to read it. Not since the 1950s and 1960s, when John Kenneth Galbraith published *The Affluent Society* and *The New Industrial State,* has an economist written a book that has garnered so much public attention and critical praise.

But the furor might have been anticipated in light of the effective way that the book taps into pre-existing worries about economic inequality. Liberals and progressives of all stripes have hailed it as the indictment of free-market capitalism they have been waiting decades to hear. The market revolutions of the past three decades have placed them on defense in public debates over taxation, regulation, and inequality, and Piketty's book provides them with the intellectual ammunition with which to fight back. It documents their belief that inequalities of income and wealth have grown rapidly in recent decades in the United States and across the industrial world, and it portrays our era as a new "gilded age" of concentrated wealth and out-of-control capitalism. It suggests that things are getting worse for nearly everyone, save for a narrow slice of the population – the "1 percent" – that lives off exploding returns on capital, and it pointedly supports their agenda of redistributive taxation.

Is Piketty a Marxist?

Some have compared *Capital in the Twenty-First Century* to Karl Marx's *Das Kapital* both for its similarity in title and its updated analysis of the historical dynamics of the capitalist system. Though Piketty deliberately chose his title to promote the association with Marx's tome, he is not a socialist or a Marxist, as he reminds the reader throughout the book. He does not endorse collective ownership of the means of production; historical materialism; class struggle; the labor theory of value; or the inevitability of revolution. He readily acknowledges that communism and socialism are failed systems. He wants to reform capitalism, not destroy it.

At the same time, he shares Marx's assumption that returns on capital are the dynamic force in modern economies, and, like Marx, he claims that such returns lead ineluctably to concentrations of wealth in fewer and fewer hands. For Piketty, like Marx, capitalism is all about "capital," and not much more. Along the same lines, he also argues that there is an intrinsic conflict between capital and labor in market systems so that greater returns on capital must come at the expense of wages and salaries. In this sense, rather like Marx, he advances an interpretation of market systems that revolves around just a few factors:

the differential returns on capital and labor and the distribution of wealth and income through the population.

Though he borrows some ideas from Marx, Piketty writes more from the perspective of a modern progressive or social democrat. His book, written in French but translated into English, bears many features of that ideological perspective, particularly in its focus on the distribution rather than the creation of wealth, in its emphasis upon progressive taxation as

---

The market revolutions of the past three decades have placed liberals on defense over taxation, regulation, and inequality, and Piketty's book provides them with the intellectual ammunition with which to fight back.

---

the solution to the inequality problem, and in the confidence it expresses that governments can manage modern economies in the interest of a more equal distribution of incomes. He is worried mainly about equality and economic security, much less so about freedom, innovation, and economic growth.

His book has some admirable features. It is, first of all, a work of economic history, a field that economists have abandoned over the past several decades in favor of building statistical models and formulating abstract theories. Piketty takes academic economists to task for the irrelevance of much of their work to the pressing problems of the day and for ignoring the lessons that history has to teach. The author takes seriously the history of economic ideas, mining the works of Adam Smith, David Ricardo, Thomas Robert Malthus, Karl Marx, and John Maynard Keynes in search of insights into the operation of the market system. He demonstrates that these theorists still have much to tell us about ongoing economic controversies, despite the fact that few economists today bother to read their works. There is much in this book to digest and reflect upon, even for those who do not share the author's point of view.

The popularity of his book is another sign that established ideas never really die but go in and out of fashion with changing circumstances. Liberals, progressives, and social democrats were shocked by the comeback of free-market ideas in the 1980s after they assumed those ideas had been buried once and for all by the Great Depression. In a similar vein, free-market and "small government" advocates are now surprised by the return of social-democratic doctrines that they assumed had been discredited by the "stagflation" of the 1970s and the success of low-tax policies in the 1980s and 1990s. Piketty's book has garnered so much attention because it is the best statement we have had in some time of the redistributionist point of view.

Despite the attention and praise the book has received, it is a flawed production in at least three important respects. First, it misjudges the era in which we are living and those through which we have passed. Second, it misunderstands the sources of the "new inequality." Third, the solutions it proposes will make matters worse for everyone – the wealthy, the middle class, and the poor alike. The broader problem with the book is that it advances a narrow understanding of the market system that singles out returns on capital as its central feature but in the process ignores the really important factors that account for its success over an extended period of 2½ centuries.

The "Iron Law" of Capitalism

Piketty organizes his book around an old question dating back to the 19th century: Does the capitalist process tend to produce over time a growing equality or inequality in incomes and wealth? In doing so he assumes without argument that equality rather than some other measure or mix of measures – such as growth, innovation, living standards, or freedom – is the basic standard according to which the system should be judged.

The dominant view throughout the 19th century was that rising inequality was an inevitable by-product of the capitalist system. In the United States, Thomas Jefferson tried to preserve an agricultural society for as long as possible in the belief that the industrial system would destroy the promise of equality upon which the new nation was based. In Great Britain, David Ricardo, writing in the early 19th century, argued that because agricultural land was scarce and finite, landowners would inevitably claim larger shares of national wealth at the expense of laborers and factory owners. Ricardo did not foresee that land prices in Great Britain would level off due to free trade and technological innovations that increased the supply and reduced the price of food.

Later, as the industrial process gained steam, Marx argued that because of competition among capitalists, ownership of capital in the form of factories and machinery would become concentrated in fewer and fewer hands, while workers continued to be paid subsistence wages. Marx did not foresee that productivity-enhancing innovations, allied perhaps with the unionization of workers, would cause wages to rise and thereby allow workers to enjoy more of the fruits of capitalism.

For Piketty, like Marx, capitalism is all about "capital," and not much more.

The perspective on the equality-inequality issue changed in the 20th century due to the rise in incomes for workers, continued improvements in worker productivity, the expansion of the service sector and the welfare state, and the general prosperity of the postwar era. In addition, the Great Depression and two world wars tended to wipe out the accumulated capital that sustained the lifestyles of the upper classes. In the 1950s, Simon Kuznets, a prominent American economist, showed that wealth and income disparities leveled out in the United States from 1913 to 1952. On the basis of his research, he proposed the so-called Kuznets curve to illustrate his conclusion that inequalities naturally increased in the early phases of the industrial process but then declined as the process matured, as workers relocated from farms to cities, and as human capital replaced physical capital as a source of income and wealth. His thesis suggested that modern capitalism would gradually produce a middle-class society in which incomes did not vary greatly from the mean. This optimistic outlook was nicely expressed in John F. Kennedy's oft-quoted remark that "a rising tide lifts all boats."

From the perspective of 2014, Piketty makes the case that Marx was far closer to being right than Kuznets. Kuznets, in Piketty's view, was simply looking at data from a short period of history and made the error of extrapolating his findings into the future.

Piketty argues that capitalism, left to its own devices and absent government intervention, creates a situation in which returns on capital grow more rapidly than returns on labor and the overall growth in the economy. This is Piketty's central point, which he takes to be a basic descriptive theorem of the capitalist order. He tries to show that when returns on capital exceed growth in the economy for many decades or generations, owners of capital disproportionately accrue wealth and income, and capital assets gradually claim larger shares of national wealth, generally at the expense of labor. This, he argues, is something close to an "iron law" of the capitalist order.

He estimates that since 1970, the market value of capital assets has grown steadily in relation to national income in all major European and North American economies. In the United States, for example, the ratio increased from almost 4 to 1 in 1970 to almost 5 to 1 today, in Great Britain from 4 to 1 to about 6 to 1, and in France from 4 to 1 to 7 to 1. Measured from a different angle, income from capital also grew throughout this period as a share of national income. From 1980 to the present, income from capital grew in the United States from 20 percent to 25 percent of the national total, in Great Britain from 18 percent to nearly 30 percent, and in France from 18 percent to about 25 percent. While these do not appear to be earthshaking changes, they weigh heavily in Piketty's narrative that stresses the outsize role that capital has seized in recent decades in relation to labor income.

The weak patterns in the data summarized above suggest that Piketty may have overstated the claims for his iron law. There is nothing particularly original or radical in the proposition that returns on capital generally exceed economic growth. Economists and investors regard it as something of a truism, at least over the long run. For example, the long-term returns on the U.S. stock market are said to be about 7 percent per annum (minus taxes and inflation), while real growth in the overall economy has been closer to 3 percent. This is generally thought to be a good thing, since returns on capital encourage greater investment, and this in turn drives innovation, productivity, and economic growth. John Maynard Keynes was not alone among prominent economists in asserting that the accumulation of capital is a measure of economic progress.

But it does not follow from this that returns on capital, even if they are greater than overall growth in incomes, must be concentrated in a few hands instead of being distributed widely in pension funds, retirement accounts, college and university endowments, individual savings, dividends, and the like. Nor is it true that greater returns on capital must come at the expense of labor, since growing productivity advances the standard of living for everyone and workers benefit along with everyone else when their savings or pensions grow with increasing returns on capital. The low and still-falling interest rates of recent decades suggest that returns for at least some forms of capital are similarly falling. It is even questionable whether wealth is in fact growing faster than incomes in the U.S. economy, as Piketty's iron law says it must do. Martin Feldstein, writing in *The Wall Street Journal*, pointed out that since 1960, household wealth in the United States has grown by 3.2 percent per year while incomes have grown at a rate of 3.3 percent per year. The reason wealth does not continue to grow permanently at a compound rate is because owners die sooner or later, at which time their assets are disbursed through estate taxes, charitable gifts, and bequests to heirs.

But why, then, has capital grown in recent decades as a share of national income and in relation to labor income? The answer is to some extent embedded in Piketty's definition of *capital*. He defines *capital* in a broad way to include not only inputs into the production process – like factories, equipment, and machinery – but also stocks, bonds, personal bank deposits, university and foundation endowments, pension funds, and residential real estate, all assets that are subject to substantial year-to-year fluctuations in market value. In his measure of capital, then, Piketty is undoubtedly incorporating the explosion in asset prices that has taken place since the early 1980s, especially in stocks and to some degree in real estate as well.

INEQUALITY AND NEW TAXES

If *Capital in the Twenty-First Century* is known for anything, it is for its documentation of rising inequality and its call for new and higher taxes on the wealthy. Every major review of the book has dwelled at length on these two subjects, often without linking them to Piketty's larger themes about the iron law of capitalism, the increasing returns on capital, and the competition between labor and capital for shares of national income. Piketty sees inequality as an inevitable by-product of modern capitalism and sees substantially higher taxes as the only means of remedying it.

There are two central chapters in the book in which he traces the distribution of wealth and incomes in the United States and Western Europe from the late 19th century to the present day. His analysis yields a series of U-shaped charts showing that the shares of wealth and income claimed by the top 1 percent or 10 percent of households peaked from 1910 to 1930, then declined and stabilized during the middle decades of the century, and then began to rise again after 1980.

In the United States in the decades before the Great Depression, the top 1 percent received about 18 percent of total income and owned about 45 percent of total wealth. Those figures fell to about 10 percent (share of income) and 30 percent (share of wealth) in the five decades from 1930 to 1980, at which point these shares started to grow again. As of 2010, the top 1 percent in the U.S. received nearly 18 percent of total incomes and owned about 35 percent of the total wealth. The pattern is similar for the top 10 percent of the income and wealth distributions. Before the Great Depression (from 1910 to 1930), this group claimed about 45 percent of national income and about 80 percent of the wealth; from 1930 to 1980, those shares fell to roughly 30 percent (income) and 65 percent (wealth); and from 1980 to 2010 their shares increased again to between 40 percent and 50 percent (income) and 70 percent (wealth). Piketty also shows that the "super-rich," the top one-tenth of 1 percent of the income distribution (about 100,000 households in 2010) increased its share of national income from about 2 percent in 1980 to close to 8 percent in 2010. The patterns are similar in the other Anglo-Saxon countries – Great Britain, Canada, and Australia – but very different in continental Europe, where the wealthiest groups have not been able to reclaim the shares of income and wealth that they enjoyed before World War I.

There is little mystery as to the sources of the U-shaped curves in income and wealth distribution in the United States and the flatter curves in continental Europe. In Europe in particular, the two great wars of the first half of the century, combined with the effects of the Great Depression, wiped out capital assets to an unprecedented degree, while progressive taxes enacted during and after World War II made it difficult for the wealthiest groups to accumulate capital at earlier rates. In the United States, the Depression wiped out owners of stocks, and high marginal income-tax rates (as high as 91 percent in the 1940s and 1950s) similarly made it difficult for "the rich" to accumulate capital. Obviously, wars, depressions, and confiscatory taxes are not beneficial to anyone, perhaps least of all to owners of capital. Beginning in the 1980s, as rates were reduced on incomes and capital gains, especially in the United States and Great Britain, those old patterns began to reappear.

Piketty highlights a new element in the situation, which is the dramatic rise in salaries for "super-managers" since the 1980s, particularly in the United States. These are, as he writes, "top executives of large firms who have managed to obtain extremely high and historically unprecedented compensation packages for their labor." This group also includes highly compensated presidents and senior executives of major colleges, universities, private foundations, and charitable institutions who often earn well in excess of $500,000 per year. Surprisingly, then, "the rich" today – the members of the top 1 percent – are salaried executives and managers rather than the "coupon clippers" of a century ago who lived off returns from stocks, bonds, and real estate. They are, in other words, people who work for a living and earn their incomes from salaries.

The solutions Piketty's book proposes will make matters worse for everyone – the wealthy, the middle class, and the poor alike.

Piketty doubts that the new super-managers earn these generous salaries on the basis of merit or contributions to business profits. He also rejects the possibility that these salaries are in any way linked to the rapidly growing stock markets of recent decades. He points instead to cozy and self-serving relationships that executives establish with their boards of directors. In a sense, he suggests, they are in a position to set their own salaries as members of a "club" alongside wealthy directors and trustees.

To remedy the growing inequality problem, Piketty advocates a return to the old regime of much higher marginal tax rates in the United States. He thinks that marginal rates could be increased to 80 percent (from 39.5 percent today) on the very rich and to 60 percent on those with incomes between $200,000 and $500,000 per year without reducing their effort in any substantial way. Such taxes would hit the so-called super-managers who earn incomes from high salaries, though it would not get at the owners of capital who take but a small fraction of their holdings in annual income.

He advocates a global "wealth tax" on the "super-wealthy," with that tax levied against assets in stocks, bonds, and real estate – though he admits that such a tax has little chance of being enacted. Wealth taxes are notoriously difficult to collect, and they encourage capital flight, hiding of assets, and disputes over the pricing of assets. They require individuals to sell assets to pay taxes, thereby causing asset values to fall. The United States has never had a wealth tax; indeed, the U.S. Constitution, while authorizing taxes on income, does not allow for taxes on wealth. Several European countries – Germany, Finland, Sweden, and others – had such a tax in the past but have discontinued it. France currently has a wealth tax that tops out at a rate of 1.5 percent on assets in excess of €10 million (or about $14 million).

Under Piketty's scheme, the tax would be imposed on a sliding scale beginning at 1 percent on modest fortunes (roughly between $1.5 million and $7 million) and perhaps reaching as high as 10 percent on "super fortunes" in excess of $1 billion. The purpose of the tax is to reduce inequality, not to spend the new revenues on beneficial public purposes. Wealthy individuals like Bill Gates and Warren Buffett, with total assets in excess of $70 billion each, might have to pay as much as $7 billion annually in national wealth taxes under such a scheme. A capital tax, according to Piketty, would have to be global in nature to guard against both capital flight and the hiding of assets in foreign accounts. It would also require a new international banking regime under which major banks would be required to disclose account information to national treasuries. In the United States, with household wealth currently at about $80 trillion, such a tax, levied even at modest rates of 1 percent or 2 percent, might yield as much as $500 billion annually.

Piketty implies that reductions in taxes over the past three decades have allowed the rich to accumulate money while avoiding paying their fair share of taxes. Nothing could be further from the truth. As income taxes and capital-gains taxes were reduced in the United States beginning in the 1980s, the share of federal taxes paid by "the rich" steadily went up. From 1980 to 2010, as the top 1 percent increased their share of before-tax income from 9 percent to 15 percent, their share of the individual income tax soared from 17 percent to 39 percent of the total paid. Their share of total federal taxes more than doubled during a period when the highest marginal tax rate was cut in half, from 70 percent to 35.5 percent. The wealthy, in short, are already paying more than their fair share of taxes, and the growth in their wealth and incomes has had nothing to do with tax avoidance or deflecting the tax burden to the middle class.

A Different Look

Piketty's estimates of wealth and income shares over the decades are probably as reliable and accurate as he or anyone else can make them, but even so, they are estimates based upon imperfect and highly inexact data often interpolated or extrapolated from entries in government records. This is especially true of his information on wealth, since governments have long maintained records on incomes (to collect taxes on them) but not on individual wealth.

Following the publication of the book, Chris Giles of the *Financial Times* double-checked some of the information on the website that Piketty maintains and in the process discovered several material errors both in the data and in Piketty's analysis. Giles writes, for example, "Professor Piketty cited a figure showing the top 10 per cent of British people held 71 per cent of total national wealth (in 2010). The Office for National Statistics' latest Wealth and Assets Survey put the figure at only 44 per cent." That is a substantial discrepancy that undercuts the claim of growing inequality in Great Britain. Giles discovered additional errors and unexplained inferences in Piketty's data on the distribution of wealth in the United States that similarly undermine his conclusions about inequality in this country. It will take some time to sort out these criticisms, as other researchers attempt to replicate his analysis and as Piketty himself replies to his critics. In the meantime, cautious readers will be justified in regarding as tentative Piketty's conclusions about rapidly growing inequalities in wealth in Great Britain and the United States.

Even where Piketty's numbers may be accurate and not subject to the above criticisms, they could still produce misleading conclusions. As some have pointed out, he uses statistics on national income as denominators for his calculations of shares of income claimed by various groups of the population, but these figures exclude transfers from the government such as Social Security payments, food stamps, rent supplements, and the like, which constitute a growing portion of income for many middle-class and working-class people. If those transfers were included in the calculations, then the shares of income claimed by the top 1 percent or 10 percent would undoubtedly decline, and the shares of other groups would increase by corresponding amounts.

Leaving this controversy aside and accepting his data as valid for the time being, there are nevertheless good reasons to question his basic conclusions about capitalism in the 20th century. Piketty claims that inequality has increased since 1980, especially in the United States and Great Britain, that this kind of inequality is built into the nature of capitalism, and that it has been exacerbated by new tax policies that have cut the levies on high incomes and great wealth. These claims are greatly exaggerated.

The inequality that he measures is essentially a by-product of the stock-market boom of the past three decades. Since the early 1980s the U.S. stock market, measured by the Dow Jones Industrial Average, has grown twentyfold, the British stock market, as measured by the FTSE 100, by nearly tenfold, and the German market (measured by the DAX 30) by more than fifteenfold. The capitalization of world stock markets has grown from about $2 trillion in 1980 to about $60 trillion today. We have lived through an unprecedented three-decade-long bull market in stocks that no one foresaw in the 1970s. It would be surprising if such an escalation in market prices did not have a significant influence on the distribution of wealth and incomes, and it would be hazardous to forecast that such a pattern must continue indefinitely into the future.

The chart on page 34 makes the point more clearly that rising inequality is closely linked to stock-market returns. The chart illustrates the strong association from 1957 to 2012 between shares of income claimed by the top 1 percent in the United States and parallel changes in the Dow Jones Industrial Average and the Standard and Poor's 500 Stock Index. The income data are taken from a paper published by Piketty and Emmanuel Saez and posted on Saez's website; the stock-market data are taken from tables published by the

Cautious readers will be justified in regarding as tentative Piketty's conclusions about rapidly growing inequalities in wealth in Great Britain and the United States.

St. Louis Federal Reserve Bank. For ease of illustration and comparison, the three measures are indexed to 100 in 1957; the values for the top 1 percent are shown on the left axis and the stock-market values are on the right. The top line – the solid black line – charts the growth in income shares of the top 1 percent, while the gray line measures changes in the S&P 500, and the dotted line changes in the Dow Jones Industrial Average.

The key point is that all three lines move along the same pattern, remaining roughly flat and stable from 1957 to 1982, then moving

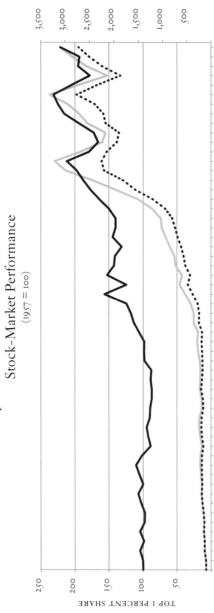

Top 1 Percent Share of National Income vs.
Stock-Market Performance
(1957 = 100)

STOCK-MARKET PERFORMANCE

—— Top 1 Percent's Share of National Income —— S&P 500 ••••• Dow Jones Industrial Average

Source: Emmanuel Saez & Thomas Picketty (http://emlberkeley.edu/~saez/); St. Louis Federal Reserve FRED

upward in tandem thereafter with peaks and valleys occurring simultaneously with booms and busts in the stock markets. The changes in inequality began to tick upward after 1980 and accelerated in the 1990s, as the stock markets gained steam. As the chart shows, income inequality dropped most rapidly and dramatically when the stock markets faltered, as they did in 2000 with the technology bust and, more spectacularly, in 2008 with the financial crisis. Measured statistically, there is a 0.95 correlation between changes in the income shares of the top 1 percent and changes in the S&P 500, and there is a 0.96 correlation with changes in the Dow Jones Industrial Average. These patterns strongly suggest that changes in inequality in the United States have been closely linked to the three-decade-long boom in world stock markets. When inequality rises as a result of a boom of this kind, it is far less socially damaging than when it is caused by a bust, as in the Great Depression.

Piketty argues that the increased compensation for super-managers in recent decades is unrelated to the impressive returns on stocks. That is a doubtful proposition, if we bear in mind that many outsize compensation packages for business executives are paid in the form of stocks and stock options. This practice was hailed a few decades ago as a means of linking an executive's performance to the success of the company, but now it is attacked because it contributes to income inequality.

One could raise the question as to why the financial markets in the United States and elsewhere suddenly took off in the early 1980s and continued their upward movement for three-plus decades. It is beyond the scope of this Broadside to offer a detailed answer to such a question. Nevertheless, a few propositions suggest themselves. The period that began in 1981 or 1982 has been one of falling interest rates and disinflation, two developments that are especially beneficial to stock and real estate prices. The elimination of trade barriers; the end of the Cold War; and the entry of China, India, and various Asian countries into the world economy were also beneficial developments that reinforced the booming stock markets but perhaps disadvantaged American workers who were now forced to compete in a global marketplace. The end of the gold standard paved the way for a rapid expansion of credit and debt in the 1980s. Cuts in tax rates played but a minor role in comparison with these more important developments.

We could, of course, "solve" the inequality problem in the same way that it was "solved" in the 1930s – by erecting trade barriers, shutting down international trade, and crashing the stock markets. Piketty does not endorse any such result – but it is one toward which his analysis indirectly points.

GILDED AGE OR GOLDEN AGE?

Professor Piketty claims – in the broader message of his book – that we are living through a new "gilded age" of extravagant wealth and lavish expenditures enjoyed by a narrow elite at the expense of everyone else. As with the original "gilded age" of the late 19th century, the wealth accrued by the few gives the illusion of progress and prosperity but conceals growing hardships and economic difficulties endured by the rest of the population. Much

We could, of course, "solve" the inequality problem in the same way that it was "solved" in the 1930s — by erecting trade barriers, shutting down international trade, and crashing the stock markets.

of his thesis rests upon this proposition: our era is one of *faux* prosperity, a claim that is manifestly untrue.

Piketty divides the history of modern capitalism into three phases: first, the original gilded age, running in Europe from roughly 1870 to the outbreak of World War I in 1914 (he often refers to it as the *Belle Époque*) and in the United States from the end of the Civil War to the stock-market crash in 1929; second, the golden age of social democracy from 1930 to 1980, when progressive tax regimes and welfare programs were installed in most industrial countries; and, third, the new gilded age beginning in 1980 and running to the present, during which these tax regimes were dismantled, marginal rates and capital-gains taxes were reduced, and wealth and income began to flow once again to the very rich. He documents these three historical phases with data and charts showing that the shares of wealth and income claimed by the top 1 percent or 10 percent of households peaked in the early decades of the 20th century, then declined and stabilized in the middle decades of the century, and then began to rise again after 1980.

This argument makes sense only if one accepts the one-eyed premise that these multifaceted regimes can be assessed on the basis of the single criterion of wealth and income distribution or that the essence of the capitalist order is found solely in returns on capital and in the distribution of wealth and incomes rather than in rising living standards, innovation, and the spread of modern civilization. In each of these three eras, there was much more going on than simply the rearranging of wealth and incomes.

No less an authority than John Maynard Keynes looked back upon the prewar era in Europe as a golden age of capitalism. "What an extraordinary episode in the economic progress of man that age was which came to an end in August, 1914," he wrote in 1919 in *The Economic Consequences of the Peace.* He marveled at the economic progress made across the continent after 1870 following the unification of Germany. Industry and population grew steadily as trade across the continent accelerated, widening the sphere of prosperity and the reach of modern comforts. In the United States, rapid growth, stable prices, and high real wages drew millions of immigrants from Europe to build railroads, work in factories, and industrialize the country. Far-reaching innovations – electricity, the telegraph, mass-produced steel, and motored cars – drove the industrial process forward and made a few people very rich. It was the first era of globalization and open trade. These three factors – innovation, migration toward emerging centers of wealth, and widening circles of trade – have been key elements of "golden ages" throughout history and especially in the modern age of capitalism. This particular golden age ended in 1914 in Europe and in 1929 in the United States.

The so-called golden age of social democracy has much to commend it; one should not gainsay the genuine economic and social progress achieved in the United States and elsewhere during the middle decades of the century. Nevertheless, the virtues of that era can be overstated. As Piketty acknowledges, much of the accumulated capital of the preceding era was wiped out by war and depression. The confiscatory tax rates of that era, with marginal rates as high as 91 percent in the U.S. in the 1940s and 1950s, played a secondary role in the relative equalization of wealth and incomes. The impressive growth rates of the 1950s and 1960s developed from a depressed base and by building out innovations from the earlier period. Labor unions grew and won impressive wage gains for members, but mainly because (in the United States) they were bargaining with domestic oligopolies in industries that included auto, steel, railroad, and aluminum. The structure of American industry was highly concentrated, which, in the opinion of some, impeded innovation. Economist Galbraith wrote that cartelization was a permanent feature of the U.S. economy. There was little immigration into the United States and Western Europe from 1930 to 1970. Most important for the distribution of wealth, the U.S. stock market barely moved in real terms from 1930 to 1980; in 1980, the Dow Jones Industrial Average was at a lower level (adjusted for inflation) than at its peak in 1929.

The high tax regime of that era collapsed in the 1970s, not because "the rich" dismantled it but because government spending and regulation brought with them more crime, dependency, and disorder, along with simultaneously growing rates of unemployment and inflation. It was Jimmy Carter who first led the charge to deregulate the airline, rail-

It may be inevitable that our "golden age" will end sooner or later – but it will be much sooner if Professor Piketty and his supporters have their way.

road, trucking, and communications industries. Democrats and Republicans alike agreed that the U.S. economy was suffering from a shortage of capital – and that tax rates should be reduced to promote capital formation. That approach succeeded, as we have seen. At the same time, U.S. leaders pushed successfully for the elimination of trade barriers and a more open international trading system.

One might echo Keynes's comments about the prewar era in Europe in reflecting upon the era through which we have lived from the 1980s to the present. Far from being a gilded age, it appears from a broader perspective to have been new golden age of capitalism, marked by life-changing innovations in technology, globalized markets, and widening circles of trade; unprecedented levels of immigration into centers of prosperity; the absence of major wars; rising living standards around the world; falling inflation and interest rates; and a 30-year bull market in stocks, bonds, and real estate. At the same time, the boom in financial assets and real estate has also enriched the endowments of colleges, universities, and foundations, along with pension and retirement funds upon which millions of households depend.

These developments broke up the concentrated structure of the U.S. economy, making it more open, competitive, and innovative. At the same time, corporate profits are far higher now than in the age of industrial concentration and oligopoly. The end of the Cold War and the entrance of China into the world economy similarly broke open the structure of world politics and finance that dominated the middle decades of the century. Meanwhile, global levels of poverty and inequality have declined dramatically over the past three decades. Though some have won incredible riches in this new age of capitalism, they have done so by developing new products and technologies that benefit everyone or by investing in enterprises that earn profits by satisfying customers.

Keynes once remarked that the challenge in such a situation is to keep the boom going, not to bring it to a premature end out of a superstition that those who have prospered must be punished. That error has been made at various times in the past, most recently in the 1930s. It may be inevitable that our "golden age" will end sooner or later – but it will be much sooner if Professor Piketty and his supporters have their way.

First American edition published in 2014 by Encounter Books, an activity of Encounter for Culture and Education, Inc., a nonprofit, tax exempt corporation.
Encounter Books website address: www.encounterbooks.com

Manufactured in the United States and printed on acid-free paper. The paper used in this publication meets the minimum requirements of ANSI/NISO Z39.48–1992 (R 1997) (*Permanence of Paper*).

FIRST AMERICAN EDITION

LIBRARY OF CONGRESS CATALOGING-IN-PUBLICATION DATA

Piereson, James.
The inequality hoax / by James Piereson.
pages   cm. — (Encounter broadsides)
ISBN 978-1-59403-785-6 (pbk. : alk. paper) — ISBN 978-1-59403-786-3 (ebook)
1. Equality. 2. Income distribution. 3. Liberalism. I. Title.
HM821.P538 2014
305—dc23
2014022018X

10 9 8 7 6 5 4 3 2 1

SERIES DESIGN BY CARL W. SCARBROUGH